Airline Interview

The Exercise Book

Interview questions and tasks from real life
selection procedures for pilots and ATCOs

SkyTest® Airline Interview – The Exercise Book

Authors: Dennis Dahlenburg, Diploma in Economic Law
                                      Andreas Gall, Diploma in Computer and Business Science

Editor: Aviation Media & IT GmbH
                                      Henkestraße 78
                                      91052 Erlangen
                                      Germany

Production and publishing: BoD - Books on Demand
                                      22848 Norderstedt, Germany

Contact: Aviation Media & IT GmbH
                                      Airline Interview
                                      Henkestraße 78
                                      91052 Erlangen
                                      Germany

Website: http://www.skytest.com

E-mail: office@skytest.com

ISBN 9783744822541

Foreword

Dear reader,

We are very pleased that you have chosen to use *SkyTest® Airline Interview – The Exercise Book* to prepare for your airline selection test. The psychological interview towards the end of a selection process ultimately decides whether a candidate will be hired as a pilot. In other words, a successful application stands and falls with the interview.

We presented the theory of interview-based suitability diagnostics for commercial pilots and air traffic controllers in our book *SkyTest® Airline Interview*. The handbook gives applicants an introduction to this interesting topic and helps them to better understand the meaning and purpose of the interview.

SkyTest® Airline Interview – The Exercise Book looks at the final part of the selection process from a practical perspective. In this book you will find the tools for targeted preparation for your upcoming interview. To succeed, you must not only avoid pitfalls, but also pick up on the intentions behind the questions and tasks posed with your responses. *SkyTest® Airline Interview – The Exercise Book* chronologically takes you through typical sections of a selection interview with an airline. The book gives you deeper insight into common interview questions. Examples and exercises will help you to respond spontaneously and confidently in future interviews.

Almost all those applying for a pilot position must discuss their qualifications and motivation at interview. This book is therefore aimed at pilots with professional experience, those who have just graduated from flight school and applicants who are still at the very start of their flight training. As the selection procedures are very similar, this book is also suitable for air traffic controllers to use in preparing for interviews.

In buying *SkyTest® Airline Interview – The Exercise Book,* you have chosen a product from the *SkyTest®* series. *SkyTest®* has been providing user-oriented training software and specialist books to help people prepare for selection tests in commercial air travel since 2003. All *SkyTest®* products are compiled with great care to see you on your way to the cockpit. We wish you every success in your recruitment test.

Erlangen, May 2017

Dennis Dahlenburg, Andreas Gall

Contents

1 Introduction

Airlines have high standards when it comes to selecting their pilots. The often multi-stage tests usually begin with a computer-based cognitive and operational performance test.

The following chart shows the characteristics often sought by airlines in their pilot selection tests:

Characteristic	Tool	Ab Initio	Ready Entry
Biographical profile	Questionnaire Application documents Telephone interview	Certificates Technical understanding	Career path Licences Type ratings Flight hours
General cognitive performance	Computer tests	Memory performance Spatial reasoning Information intake and processing Logical reasoning Ability to concentrate	
Profession-specific cognitive performance	Computer tests	Repetitive work Psychomotor activity Attention distribution Situational attention	
Operational skills	Computer tests Simulator tests	Decision-making behaviour Planning behaviour Strategic problem solving Prioritisation of tasks	

Table 1: Basic aptitude evaluation

Applicants who have demonstrated their basic suitability for the pilot profession will then be invited to undergo subsequent psychological tests with an interview. In the past, these interviews were more focused on technical and theoretical topics. However, modern selection processes go deeper. Today, the interview should not just provide information about *qualifications,* but more about the applicant's *motivation* and *probable future behaviour* in their intended work environment.

Reaching the interview means you have made it to a select pool of applicants. The airline is now particularly interested in seeing the applicant's social skills and personality-related characteristics.

Characteristic	Tool	Ab Initio	Ready Entry
Social skills	Group exercises Computer tests Interview	Team behaviour Strong communication skills Assertiveness	Conflict prevention Conflict resolution Leadership skills Hierarchy behaviour
Personality-related characteristics	Interview	Motivation for becoming a pilot Career motivation vs. leisure orientation Discipline Taking responsibility Ability to work in regulated systems Ability to self-assess Dealing with stress triggered by • high work load • social environment • professional environment • time pressure	

Table 2: Psychological suitability assessment and interview

Various approaches have been developed and optimised for use by airlines in order to carry out the psychological suitability assessment and interview. As a rule, airlines carry out what are known as *half-structured, mixed interviews*, which essentially follow an internal guide and progress on the basis of biographical and situational questions. As part of the selection process, the interview is regularly accompanied by psychological analytical methods, such as group exercises or computer tests. The supplementary tests are there to ensure the results of the final interview are correct.

We examined the theoretical approaches behind the methods of interview-based selection diagnostics in pilot tests and their practical implementation in selection processes in the *SkyTest® Airline Interview* book. *SkyTest® Airline Interview – The Exercise Book* was specifically developed for the purpose of targeted preparation for meeting the interviewer.

The book will help you to find answers to possible questions about your professional career or biographical background *before the interview.* The verbal and syntactic presentation of your answers during interview is at least as important as confident content preparation. There are notes on this in the individual chapters of this book.

2 Before the interview

Invitation to interview requires more than just successful participation in any cognitive and operational performance tests. You must also pass two formal hurdles – the written application and, in many cases, a preliminary telephone interview.

2.1 Application letter and CV

The application letter is the first impression the airline's HR department gets of an applicant. Your covering letter should be no more than one page of A4 and your attached CV should provide all the essential information about your qualifications and experience. The covering letter should also convey that you are a motivated employee with good social skills who will integrate well into a new team. You can achieve a good blend of conveying information and motivation using the following structure:

First paragraph: Your current situation and motivation

A good introduction to a covering letter sent to an airline is a detailed description of your current employment status and collected flight experience. You should outline why you have applied to this particular airline in the last sentence of the first paragraph.

Applicants applying for flight training roles should describe their current professional or educational situation in the introduction, and then go into detail about why they have chosen to become a pilot.

Second paragraph: Your aviation training and qualifications

Stages of training, licences, flight hours on individual routes and simulator experience all belong in the second paragraph. The focus here is purely on getting the information across.

Third paragraph: Training and career outside the cockpit

Academic degrees and professional roles outside of the aircraft cockpit can be covered in the third paragraph.

Fourth paragraph: Professional ethics and social skills

You should end your covering letter by showing your positive and professional attitude towards being a pilot and by emphasising your social skills. You may also refer to activities you undertake in your spare time.

2.2 Example: Covering letter for a pilot position

Subject: Application as a First Officer in your B737 fleet

Dear Sir/Madam,

I am writing to apply for a role as a First Officer in your Boeing 737 fleet. I am single, 30 years old and currently live in Melbourne, where I have been flying the 737-800 as a F/O for Jetstar for the last two years. Before this, I spent four years flying ambulance flights for the Royal Flying Doctor Service of Australia (RFDS) on a Beechcraft Super King 200C. I gained a lot of valuable experience from my time with RFDS. I learnt to react flexibly and make quick decisions on flights in difficult weather conditions, in night operations at unknown airfields and during emergencies in the care of patients on board. As a pilot for the RFDS, I was responsible for planning the deployment, preparation and tanking of aircraft, as well as instructing new crew members. These experiences made it far easier for me to move over to commercial air travel. My contract with Jetstar will end this September. After it ends, I would like to return back to Europe after my time in Australia. I would like to continue my career with your airline, as I would enjoy being part of a company and environment that opens up new opportunities for me.

I completed my flight training in June 2006 at the Hamburg flight school. I have a current ATPL with Commercial Pilot and Multi-Engine certificates. I passed the ATPL theoretical tests with an average of 94.5 percent. Including 200 hours of multi-crew training in the simulator, I have 2,100 hours of flight experience, of which 1,200 were spent on the 737 NG.

Before my flying career, I completed a degree in Business Management with a focus on aviation at the University of Hamburg. I completed my Bachelor of Arts (BA) degree with an average grade of 1.8 after six semesters. After completing my degree, I worked for a year as a trainee at Airbus in Hamburg and Toulouse before I decided on a career in aviation. I learnt a lot about business management, customer relations and finance in the multi-faceted Airbus trainee programme.

I like being a pilot because I value working as part of a team. I am responsible and reliable when it comes to taking on leadership tasks. Safety and professionalism are the principles of my work in the cockpit and when preparing to fly. I strive to live a balanced lifestyle in my free time. I learnt to play cricket in Australia and have been training a youth team for a year on a voluntary basis. I am convinced that my qualifications and social skills would make me a valuable employee at your airline.

With thanks and best regards,

...

Your CV is attached to the covering letter. The most important information about you, your qualifications and roles from your career and training should be highlighted on your CV.

1. Header

You can put your qualification "highlights" in bullet points in the header of your CV.

2. Personal information

Your personal information should include:

- Name
- Address
- Telephone number
- Email address
- Date of birth
- Nationality
- Native language
- Foreign languages
- Medical

3. Flying experience

Give the airline a brief overview of your flight experience. This overview should include:

- Flight time
  - ☐ Total flight time with a simulator
  - ☐ Total flight time without a simulator
  - ☐ PIC
  - ☐ IFR
  - ☐ Piston / Jet

■ Types of aircraft flown (include information on flight hours for each)

4. Professional career

List professional roles you have held chronologically, starting with your most recent (current) role. Of the information provided, you should highlight:

■ Period of employment
■ Job title
■ Role description
■ Name and address of employer

5. Aviation and non-aviation training

The last section of your CV should list your education details. Again, list in chronological order, starting with the last place you studied. You should highlight:

■ Training period
■ Flight school / institute / university
■ Training content / focus
■ Graduation

6. Date and signature!

2.3 Preliminary telephone conversation

Most airlines arrange a brief telephone conversation with applicants being considered for employment or training. This is a (small) interview in and of itself. They will decide whether or not to invite you to further recruitment tests during the ten to twenty minute conversation.

You should expect them to *fact check*. This means that during the telephone call you should keep in mind the information provided on your application (particularly things such as flight hours, training or career roles and, if relevant, any findings from prior aeromedical examinations).

The telephone call generally has a relaxed feel to it. You will not be confronted with overly critical questions on the phone. However, you should avoid it becoming too chatty. Answer competently, precisely and fully, but above all, remain friendly. Always allow your conversation partner to finish speaking.

You should take the call in a room where you will not be distracted and where there is no disruptive background noise. Having the conversation while sat at a desk is ideal.

You will be asked questions on the phone which you will then have to answer again during the in-person interview. Classic questions include:

- What is the reason for your application?

- What do you know about our company?

- Why would you like to work for us?

- Tell us a bit about your career to date.

- What experience will you bring to our company?

- When can you start?

- Would you describe yourself as being reliable?

- Have you ever had a conflict with a supervisor during your career?

The backgrounds to these questions and strategies for preparing your answers will be covered in the upcoming chapters. You should briefly write down the answers you provide on the phone. Answers provided on the phone to the same or similar questions must not contradict things you later say at interview.

The interviewer will discuss the next stages of the process with you at the end of the telephone call. You will not usually receive an immediate invitation to attend a further interview. However, you will be informed of when and how you can expect to receive feedback. Thank the person for calling and then start to prepare for a personal meeting with an airline representative.

The day of the interview has come. Approach it with a positive attitude. The interview does not start with the first question, but rather as soon as you enter the building. Be friendly yet professional with all employees and fellow applicants – the receptionist could have just as much say in deciding for or against an applicant as the HR Manager.

The goal is to distinguish yourself from the other applicants. This is achieved by avoiding the (formal) pitfalls that some applicants fall into:

- Arrive in immaculate formal **clothing** – a dark suit and tie for men or a business suit for women. Arriving in the uniform of a former (or worse, current) employer, is a real taboo.

- Greet the airline employee with a **firm handshake**, maintain eye contact. Show approachable body language. A smile will not hurt.

- **Maintain concentration.** A lack of concentration is evident, for example, when you have to ask about something that has already been explained to you.

- **Do not make jokes.** You are in the professional recruitment process for a job which entails a great deal of responsibility.

- **Do not be arrogant.** Even if you used to work as a fleet commander for a large airline; arrogance when dealing with recruiters significantly reduces your chances of being hired.

- (Positive) **small talk** amongst applicants is allowed.

- Always use **professional language**. *"Where can I get something to eat around here?"* is not the right way to ask about the canteen at lunch time.

- Turn your **mobile phone** to silent or off.

- Show **composure.** Restless pacing in the waiting room does not calm you down and does not draw a good picture of how you handle stressful situations.

- Always use your **common sense!**

The interview is held in a neutrally decorated room. There will usually be between one and four recruitment staff members present. Not all of them will take an active role in the conversation: some are there to observe your behaviour and take notes. Try to use eye contact to respond to all participants, even those who are not actively taking part. You should not expect reactions from them, such as an acknowledging nod. Do not allow this to unsettle you.

By reaching the interview you are down to the final ten percent of the original applicant pool. The next 45 to 90 minutes decide whether you can compete against the rest. This is, of course, always relative. Use the interview to present yourself in the best and most professional light.

3 The interview

There is no *interview template.* Each interview is specially tailored and prepared to suit the individual applicant. The basis for this is the application documents submitted and the behaviour or performance of the candidate in the selection process thus far.

Nevertheless, the interview will be based on a basic framework that is divided into four sections:

1. Reason for motivation

The start of the interview is reserved for questions regarding your motivation for becoming a pilot and your application.

2. Behavioural prediction

The second important part of the interview poses *biographical* or *situational/scenario-based* questions. These are used to predict the applicant's future behaviour within the structures and processes of their future work environment. A positive or negative behavioural forecast has the highest weighting in selecting candidates and is now as important as an applicant's qualifications.

3. Technical questions

Questions on (flight) technical specialist knowledge allow the airline to test the applicant's professional qualifications. You must not show any weakness here. This round of the interview is ultimately an investigation of your theoretical knowledge. This should of course not be limited to physics and technology; you should also update your knowledge of human performance and limitations theory and aviation law before the interview. Interviewers often spice up the conversation with targeted questions in these fields.

4. Asking the airline questions

"Do you have any questions for us?" Those who say no miss the opportunity to once again emphasise their motivation for the advertised role by asking their own questions.

We will look at these four sections of the interview in detail on the following pages. The examples and exercises should help you to prepare for the interview. Tip: answer the exercises with bullet points which will later be used to verbally formulate your answer. Having answers prepared can lead you to anticipate questions. You should avoid this. In the interview you must demonstrate your (verbal) flexibility. Always let the interviewer finish! *"Give me an example of a disagreement you have had with a colleague"* is a different task to *"Give me an example of a disagreement you had with a colleague that you managed to win in your favour"*. It is not bad to have brief pauses in the conversation. On the contrary, this will show the interviewer that you are thinking about your answer. You would be expected to do the same in the cockpit.

3.1 Reason for motivation

You will be asked about your motivation for becoming a pilot and your application at the start of a half-structured interview. This part of the interview is particularly good as an introduction to the conversation, as you can see from the typical introductory questions.

3.1.1 Shall we start by you telling me a bit about yourself?

This question is a classic *opener* in the interview. At first glance, this question seems quite harmless. It gives the interviewer their first impression on whether

- you answer in a structured and comprehensive way,

- and whether you have identified a motivation for becoming a pilot using your biographical information.

Correspondingly, you should focus your answer on your professional career (without simply regurgitating your entire CV, which the interviewer is already familiar with). There is a four-stage process to tackling this question:

1. Start with your private background (family status, hobbies)

2. Talk about what made you interested in flying (motivation!)

3. Talk about your education and career

4. End with talking about your current career

One of the most important rules for the interview is: **Give the interviewer information!** Interviewers do not like having to drag every detail out of the applicant. Your answers should provide valuable additional information.

Make sure your answer always has a **positive tone**! You want to show yourself to be motivated and above all independent and responsible. A failed checkride? – "I made a second attempt not long after and passed" is a better answer than, "I thought my performance was good, but the Captain didn't want to let me pass from the outset".

Always show yourself to be **future and opportunity-oriented**! Have you only flown freight so far? *"I look forward to flying airline passengers to their destination"* is a better answer than *"So far, I have only had experience with cargo"*.

This also applies to former roles: look back **positively** on your time with former employers. Keep a lid on it (until you are in the new cockpit, of course). You can briefly refer to roles outside of aviation or simply leave them on your CV.

If there is something very unique or exceptional about your biography, you should certainly mention it. This makes you easier to remember when the interviewers are discussing your application during the selection process (*"that was the person who had a student job as a laughter yoga teacher...", "that was the mountain climber...").*

An answer to the question "Shall we start by you telling me a bit about yourself?" could for example be:

"99

> *My name is David Müller, I currently live in Amsterdam and recently turned 31. I have been married for two years and have a one-year-old daughter. I keep myself fit for my family and my job by cycling and surfing.*
>
> *At 16 I tutored younger students to finance my glider flying lessons. This is what led me to aviation.*
>
> *I completed my ATPL at the end of 2004 at the Aachen flight school. As I unfortunately didn't find a role with an airline immediately afterwards, I worked at a theatre box office while applying for roles. I have been working at Tulip Airlines in the Netherlands for six years and fly the CRJ-900 as a F/O regionally. I am very happy with my job but would like to continue my career as a F/O in your 737 fleet.*

Exercise

Write an answer to the question "Shall we start by you telling me a bit about yourself?"

But be careful not to memorise your text! All your answers in the interview have to be spontaneous. The interviewer must not get the impression that you are reeling off a well-prepared answer from your mind's eye. Avoid pretentious grammar or phrases and focus more on the type of conversation you would have when talking with a friend.

3.1.2 What made you apply to our airline?

Every applicant in every company is asked this question. However, it is rarely answered well. To do so, you must only credibly convey that you researched the airline beforehand and that your application is serious. Some interviewers are even more direct: *"What do you know about our company?"* or *"Why do you want to work for us?"*

You should talk less about yourself and more about the airline in your response. This is relatively straightforward – prepare two *bullet points* on what you believe makes the company the perfect employer for you:

1. Gather facts about the airline

All the information you need can be found online. You can also often download the current annual report of publicly listed airlines from their Investor Relations page, providing you with valuable information. Try to identify the airline's unique features that positively differentiate them from their competitors and highlight these during the interview.

Facts that you should memorise:

- Which aircraft are used?
- Where are the hubs and focal points of the network?
- What is the airline's current profit situation?
- What awards has the airline received recently?
- What are the names of the airline's most important managers?
- How many (flight) staff are employed by the airline?
- Is the airline a member of an alliance? Who are their most important cooperative partners?

2. Evaluate the airline as an employer

This is not an easy task. During the interview, you have to emphasise that the airline is the right fit for you and vice versa. An airline's organisation does little to adapt to their pilots. **On the contrary, (new) pilots have to integrate well into the existing processes and systems and show a willingness to be flexible.** When you evaluate the airline as an employer, therefore, no more than one quarter of your evaluation should relate to your requirements for an employer. Three quarters should comprise arguments you have found to show why the airline's work environment is ideal for you.

Starting points for evaluating the airline as an employer:

- Motivated and professional workforce
- Good reputation as an employer
- Career and promotion opportunities
- Training and qualification programmes "on the job"
- Varied, international deployment
- Corporate lifestyle

Avoid talking about the salary, social benefits or holidays. The airline should not perceive these points to be your motivation for applying. A safe workplace, however, is an argument that the airline likes to hear.

An answer to the question, "What made you apply to our airline?" could, for example, be:

""

"I want to work for your airline because it presents itself internally and externally as an innovative and sustainable company. Despite the difficult market conditions, you were able to generate an operating profit of 800 million euros last year.

Your airline has over 230 aircraft – from the CRJ900 to the Airbus A380. Your flights are, on average, over 80 percent filled to capacity. In the coming years you expect to take on 40 new medium and long-haul aircraft and increase your seating capacity by 15 percent. This shows me that young pilots could have long-term and diverse career prospects with your airline.

Your airline was recently awarded by IATA for its exceptional crew training. Your workforce is young, international, professional and friendly. I would be delighted to be part of this team and know that I would enjoy working for your airline every day. Your pilots appear very happy and motivated. Passengers also regularly give your airline top marks. I would be very proud to be able to shape the rest of my career in this environment and be stationed at your international hubs during this time. It is this conviction that ultimately motivated me to apply for the role."

Exercise

Provide the following information about the airline you are applying to:

■ **Key facts about the company's history**

■ **Board and management staff**

■ **Current profit situation and business performance over the last three years**

■ **Hubs and current priority areas in the network (e.g. tourism, charter business and business travel)**

■ **Planned development of network and frequencies**

■ **Current traffic figures and traffic development over the last three years (especially ASK, RPK and passenger figures)**

■ **Alliances and partnerships (e.g. codeshares)**

■ **Current fleet structure**

_____

_____

_____

_____

■ **Fleet development in the coming years**

_____

_____

_____

_____

■ **Workforce structure (especially qualification levels, internationality)**

_____

_____

_____

_____

■ **Staff development and career programmes**

_____

_____

_____

_____

■ **Communicated corporate culture**

_____

_____

_____

_____

■ **Current marketing and image campaigns**

_____

_____

_____

_____

■ **Awards and unique selling points**

_____

_____

_____

_____

3.1.3 Why should we hire you?

In the last question it was three quarters about the airline and just one quarter about yourself. Now it is all about you and your ability to sell yourself!

Be careful: Many interviewers phrase the question so as to challenge the applicant – "We have already seen five applicants today who all have more experience and a better CV than you. So why should we hire you?" The question can also be more neutral – "What do you think are your personal strengths?" or "How would a colleague describe you?"

You can easily make this question more tangible by identifying **verifiable characteristics** that convey your value to the airline. Think less about your qualifications – the airline can already find this information in your application documents. It is more interesting to them to hear about personal attributes that show you to be a reliable, hardworking and motivated employee.

Exercise

The following are some examples of characteristics. Look for ways to emphasise that you possess these characteristics – ideally in the context of your aviation career to date:

■ **Team player**

....

....

....

....

■ **Reliable**

....

....

....

....

■ **Positive attitude**

....

....

....

....

■ **Determined**

....

....

....

....

■   **Dedicated**

_____

_____

_____

_____

■   **Respectful**

_____

_____

_____

_____

■   **Flexible**

_____

_____

_____

_____

■   **Honest**

_____

_____

_____

_____

■   **Calm**

_____

_____

■ **Compassionate**

■ **Strong leader**

■ **Skilled communicator**

■ **Even-tempered**

■ **Loyal**

■ **Patient**

■ **Future-oriented**

■ **Responsible**

■ **Unbiased**

- **Cooperative**

- **Open-minded**

3.1.4 Follow-up questions

Your responses will always give an attentive interviewer a starting point for asking follow-up questions. Follow-up questions are targeted and require a **brief and precise answer.**

The interviewer will often address sensitive areas using interposed questions. Consider the interviewer's intention in asking such questions – he or she does not want to embarrass you, but simply wishes to obtain information about how you handled a situation. *Win the interviewer over with facts!* This can be illustrated in the following examples:

Example 1

Question: *So you're applying with us while employed by one of our competitors. What do you dislike about your current workplace?*

Intention: This question is directly related to the motivation behind your planned change of workplace.

Tip: Questions about former work relationships (or parallel applications!) are a minefield. Derogatory remarks about a former employer (or a competitor) or worse, about former colleagues, are a real taboo at interview. This shows the interviewer a lack of loyalty or teamwork. Always be positive and future-oriented!

Answer: *My former employer gave me a very good start to my career in aviation. However, there will not be any Captain programmes in the airline in the next few years due to restructuring. Even though I regret leaving such a good team, now is the right time for me to continue my career within the structure of a larger airline.*

Example 2

Question: *According to your CV, after being dismissed from your former employer you were not employed by an airline from December 2009 to September 2010. That was the period of economic upswing. Why were you fired and why did it take you nine months to find a new position?*

Intention: Being laid off and periods of unemployment are not uncommon in a cyclical industry like commercial aviation. The interviewer is not asking you this question to embarrass you. He or she simply wants to see what you did during that time and what that says about your character and attitude towards being a pilot.

Tip: Do not try to justify negative points on your CV. Explain what initiative you took.

Answer: *My employer had to file for bankruptcy in autumn 2009. As soon as it was clear that pilots would be laid off, I started to expand my qualifications outside of the CRJ craft I had previously flown. In the following months I prepared for a type rating for the A320. In June 2010 this helped me to get a new work contract that would start in the September. During my period of unemployment, I taught tennis lessons to keep myself fit and earn some money.*

(It is of course somewhat more difficult to discuss being dismissed due to behavioural or disciplinary action. This is a real black spot on any CV. In these cases you will not gain any trust if you try to justify yourself or shift the responsibility on to others. Look to the future and show that you have grappled with the former situation and learnt from it.)

Weaknesses

If you are asked about your strengths, it is obvious that you will also be asked to assess your own **weaknesses**. Of course you have weaknesses – the interviewer does not ask about your weaknesses just to hear that you have none.

Lots of applicants exaggerate a strength to the extreme to make it sound like a weakness (*"I can be very, very meticulous with my work and am a perfectionist"*). Do not do this, as to do so is to miss the intention behind the question. The interviewer primarily wants to find out whether you recognise a certain characteristic to be a weakness. They are particularly interested in a) why you see this trait as a weakness and b) how you deal with it or what you are doing to rectify this weakness.

It is also bad to only list *lack of qualifications* as your weakness. This does not tell the interviewer anything about your personality. They are also often irrelevant. If you, as a pilot, are not fluent in French then this can perhaps be a weakness but not a big problem (unlike a lack of English skills).

"Good" weaknesses for the interview can be derived from your strengths.

Strengths	Possible derived weakness
Strong communication skills	Speaking before you think
Open-minded	Sometimes too trusting
Team player	Blindly relying on others
High identification with the pilot profession	Relying solely on your career for self-affirmation

Table 3: Potential strengths and their derived weaknesses

You always walk a thin line when discussing your own weaknesses. This makes it all the more important to not just limit your answer to naming your weaknesses, but also to

■ recognise why these traits are a problem or have even caused problems in the past, and

■ conclude with ways in which you currently work on or have worked on getting rid of the weakness in question.

A weakness should not be an acute problem. You must show the interviewer that you do not simply accept the weakness, but want to improve it. Nothing demonstrates self-awareness and a willingness to change better than a problematic trait that you successfully work to eliminate:

"In the past I often used to take a backseat when working in a team. This led to others presenting my work as their own. Since becoming aware of this problem I have tried to take an active role, even in larger teams."

or

> *"I am not very good at saying "no" to people. This meant I was often taken advantage of. I have since learnt to trust my gut and don't simply do favours for others out of the goodness of my heart."*

You have free rein when choosing your examples. However, a poorly chosen example of a weakness can quickly rule you out of the interview. A real red flag are weaknesses which show a (unintentional) lack of motivation – you should not be *"a bit lazy sometimes"* nor should you put off tasks to the last minute. The interview is not the place to come clean about your worst character traits. If in doubt, look for weaknesses an employer can cope with – especially if you have already found a solution to handle the problem yourself.

Exercise

Identify and describe five personal weaknesses.

■ **1st weakness / negative trait:**

_____

_____

_____

_____

■ **Why this is a weakness:**

_____

_____

_____

_____

■ **What problems has this weakness led to / could this weakness lead to:**

_____

_____

....
....

■ **What am I doing to counteract this weakness / could I do to counteract this weakness:**

....
....
....
....

■ **2nd weakness / negative trait:**

....
....
....
....

■ **Why this is a weakness:**

....
....
....
....

■ **What problems has this weakness led to / could this weakness lead to:**

....
....
....
....

▨ **What am I doing to counteract this weakness / could I do to counteract this weakness:**

▨ **3rd weakness / negative trait:**

▨ **Why this is a weakness:**

▨ **What problems has this weakness led to / could this weakness lead to:**

■ **What am I doing to counteract this weakness / could I do to counteract this weakness:**

_____

_____

_____

_____

■ **4th weakness / negative trait:**

_____

_____

_____

■ **Why this is a weakness:**

_____

_____

_____

■ **What problems has this weakness led to / could this weakness lead to:**

_____

_____

_____

_____

■ **What am I doing to counteract this weakness / could I do to counteract this weakness:**

_____

■ **5th weakness / negative trait:**

■ **Why this is a weakness:**

■ **What problems has this weakness led to / could this weakness lead to:**

■ **What am I doing to counteract this weakness / could I do to counteract this weakness:**

3.2 Behavioural prediction

In addition to ascertaining an applicant's motivation, the prediction of their future behaviour is the second most important aspect of the interview. As part of behavioural prediction, the interviewers are investigating two personality traits that are the most important from the airline's perspective: **Reliability** and **professionalism**.

Predictions about future work behaviour can already be made by looking at *biographical* features. For example, a CV with a seamless succession of roles in education and professional positions demonstrates the applicant's high level of determination and individual responsibility both now and in the future. Even a small detail – for example, the choice of a certain advanced course at school – can be used for biographically-based behavioural predictions.

Time is put aside for *situational* and *scenario-based* questions in modern interviews in order to supplement and ensure the veracity of the biographical behavioural predictions. Interview participants are asked to describe their behaviour in certain situations. The question can either be an actual experience the applicant has gone through or a hypothetical scenario.

This part of the interview requires particularly thorough preparation. You must not only find suitable (= aviation-related) examples for typical scenarios, but also take a presentation formula for the selected examples with you into the interview.

You can expect to be asked questions relating to these four behavioural areas:

▦ Decision-making and planning

▦ Communication and conflict behaviour

▦ Behaviour under stress and ability to handle monotony

▦ Teamwork and leadership behaviour

3.2.1 Decision-making and planning

Every flight requires pilots to make new decisions. Questions about safety, efficiency and the flight organisation have to be systematically prepared for or, if in doubt, answered spontaneously in a split second. In the interview you have to prove that you can weigh up alternative actions quickly and systematically and then make a confident decision.

Exercise

Answer the following questions (choose situational examples from your career in aviation):

- What were the three most difficult decisions I have ever had to make?

  - [ ] What alternatives did I have to choose from?
  - [ ] How did I reach my final decision?

- When have I had to make very spontaneous decisions?

  - [ ] Do I react systematically or intuitively to fast decisions?

- Do I have a different approach for making decisions with long-term effects?

- In which situations did I have to make a decision before a deadline?

- When have I made the wrong decision?

  - [ ] How did I recognise this error and correct it?
  - [ ] What have I learnt from this wrong decision?

3.2.2 Communication and conflict behaviour

Every interaction between pilots in the cockpit requires communication skills. Communication between pilots and air traffic controllers is just as important for safety as communication on board. Communication is so important in the aviation industry that there are international rules and standards governing it (see, for example, *ICAO Standard Phraseology*).

The forms of standardised communication are part of the education and professional training of commercial pilots and air traffic controllers. Individual communication behaviour should be subordinate to standardised communication. However, standardised communication reaches its limit when dealing with a conflict arising over a decision. The further development of the situation now depends on whether (and how) the conflict can be resolved. During the interview you will therefore invariably be asked questions that focus on your communication skills in conflict situations.

Exercise

Answer the following questions (choose situational examples from your career in aviation):

- Which minor or major conflict situations have I been involved in?

  - [ ] How did I behave in these conflict situations?
  - [ ] How did I try to help resolve the conflicts?
  - [ ] How did the conflicts end?

■ Was I ever the cause/trigger of conflict situations?

 ☐ How did I behave in these conflict situations?
 ☐ How did I try to contribute to the resolution of the conflict?
 ☐ How did the conflicts end?

■ Have I ever had to mediate a conflict between two colleagues?

 ☐ How did I behave in these conflict situations?
 ☐ How did I try to help resolve the conflicts?
 ☐ How did the conflicts end?

■ Have there been conflict situations that I could not resolve?

■ What roles did hierarchies play in the conflicts?

■ How would colleagues, friends or family members describe my behaviour in conflict situations?

3.2.3 Behaviour under stress and ability to handle monotony

Stress has a decisive influence on both our decision-making ability and our communication behaviour. Stress can either arise suddenly (e.g. in an emergency situation) or become noticeable as a result of long-term strain (e.g. in the form of decreasing concentration levels). A persistent lack of stress (monotony) can have just as negative an effect on personal performance as stress.

As stress and boredom are both key cockpit safety factors, the interviewers will examine both your stress behaviour and your ability to handle monotony.

Exercise

Answer the following questions (choose situational examples from your career in aviation):

■ What environmental factors cause me to feel stressed?

■ How do I react to long-term strain (e.g. insomnia, fatigue)?

■ How do I react to sudden stress (e.g. passivity, being overtaxed, but also: increased attention demands, adrenaline rush)?

■ When was I spontaneously exposed to stress?

 ☐ What influence did the stress have on my decision-making and communication behaviour?
 ☐ How did the situation end?

■ How quickly do I decrease my stress levels?

▧ How do I counteract long-term stress in my free time (e.g. through sport, hobbies)?

▧ What situations bore me?

  ☐ What influence does boredom have on my decision-making and communication behaviour?
  ☐ How do I motivate myself in boring work processes?

3.2.4 Teamwork and leadership behaviour

Flying is a very complex form of teamwork. For a successful flight, several individual teams have to work effectively together, both internally and with teams from other areas at the same time. These teams do not just include cockpit and cabin crew. The staff on the ground (e.g. at the desk, in maintenance or dispatch) play a large role in successful aircraft flight.

As the pilot, you have a key role in the overall organisation, because after all, lots of threads come together in the cockpit. In addition to being able to work in a (hierarchical and organisationally regulated) team, individual leadership ability is an important qualification for a pilot to have – airlines are looking for potential Captains. A boss says "go", a good team leader says "let's go".

Exercise

Answer the following questions (choose situational examples from your career in aviation):

▧ In which situations am I regularly part of a team?

▧ What tasks have I had to solve in a two-man team (e.g. an emergency situation in the cockpit or challenging route planning)?

▧ What was the hierarchy of this team?

  ☐ How did I contribute to problem-solving?
  ☐ How did the situation end?

▧ What tasks have I had to solve in teams of more than two people?

  ☐ What was the hierarchy of this team?
  ☐ How did I contribute to problem-solving?
  ☐ How did the situation end?

▧ Which leadership positions have I already held?

▧ Have I ever had to take over a leadership role within a team spontaneously or when unprepared?

▧ How would colleagues describe my leadership style?

- ▩   What mistakes have I made in leadership positions?

- ▩   How was I made aware of these mistakes?

- ▩   What have I learnt from these mistakes?

- ▩   Has my leadership behaviour changed over time?

3.2.5 Handling situational questions

Handling situational questions in a skilful way is no easy task. In the previous exercises you were required to remember experiences that you could then use in your answers. The interviewer is simply asking applicants with flight experience to draw on their real-life experiences. You should not be short of examples you can use to illustrate your behaviour in the interview.

Be careful: Only choose authentic examples from your own wealth of experience! The interviewer examines several hundred pilots a year. What impression will he or she get of an applicant who describes the exact same situation from a reference book as two other candidates before him or her on the same day?

You should of course choose aviation-related examples in the interview. However, the chosen situation is only of minor importance – most pilots are faced with similar tasks and conflicts during their careers. What is more important is to give the interviewer information about how you *handled the situation* and the *result*. You should use the following formula when answering situational questions:

- ▩   Description of the situation   (1/4)

- ▩   How I handled the situation   (2/4)

- ▩   Result / resolution of the situation   (1/4)

By using this simple structure to construct your answer, you help both the interviewer and yourself by avoiding getting weighed down in (unnecessary) details and ultimately losing your train of thought. In line with the proposed weighting, the clear focus of your answer should be describing how you handled your chosen situation.

Description of the situation: 1/4

Talk like a pilot! Limit yourself to a chronological account of the essential facts and do not bore the interviewer with an overly detailed description. A concise but complete summary of the flow of events is a good introduction to answering a situational question. Get to the key point quickly:

How I handled the situation: 2/4

The situational questions are used to predict future behaviour. Show the interviewer that you can convey information well and single out the highlights of your behaviour. The way you handled the situation should of course show authority and professionalism.

Result / resolution of the situation: 1/4

Do you like films that leave the audience wondering what happened at the end? A story is incomplete without a conclusion. The interviewer should not be left wondering *"what happened next?"* at the end of your answer.

Example

You are given the following task during the interview: *"Describe a crisis situation that you have experienced in the cockpit."*

1. Description of the situation

> *I was the co-pilot on an Airbus A320 on a ferry flight from Hamburg to Frankfurt without any passengers on board. Shortly after take-off, the Captain had a severe nosebleed and complained of a headache. He declared himself no longer able to fly.*

2. How I handled the situation

> *I told him that we would immediately fly to the nearest airport in Hannover. I then declared an emergency and asked the tower in Hannover for preferential landing and medical assistance on the ground. The Captain's condition was of great concern to me, as he was clearly suffering from a very severe headache. I tried not to let him see my tension and kept him informed about our current position. At the same time I went through the checklist for landing, made a safe approach to Hannover and conducted a safe landing.*

3. Result / resolution of the situation

66 99

> *After landing we were directed to a parking position where there was already an ambulance waiting for us. Once the Captain was in the hands of the paramedics, I informed the airline about the incident. The Captain thanked me a few days later and praised my professional behaviour. We were happy to fly together later on.*

Exercise

Write structured responses to the following questions / tasks:

■ **When have you had to make a quick decision?**

☐ Description of the situation

....

....

....

....

☐ How I handled the situation

....

....

....

....

☐ Result / resolution of the situation

....

....

....

....

▤ **Tell me about a mistake you have made in the cockpit.**

☐ Description of the situation

_____

_____

_____

_____

☐ How I handled the situation

_____

_____

_____

_____

☐ Result / resolution of the situation

_____

_____

_____

_____

▤ **What has been the most difficult decision you have had to make up to now?**

☐ Description of the situation

_____

_____

_____

_____

☐   How I handled the situation

_____

_____

_____

_____

☐   Result / resolution of the situation

_____

_____

_____

_____

■   **Give me an example of how you prioritise tasks.**

☐   Description of the situation

_____

_____

_____

_____

☐   How I handled the situation

_____

_____

_____

_____

☐ Result / resolution of the situation

_____

_____

_____

_____

▨ **Tell me about a conflict with a supervisor.**

☐ Description of the situation

_____

_____

_____

_____

☐ How I handled the situation

_____

_____

_____

_____

☐ Result / resolution of the situation

_____

_____

_____

_____

■ **Tell me about a conflict with a colleague of equal standing to yourself.**

☐   Description of the situation

_____

_____

_____

_____

☐   How I handled the situation

_____

_____

_____

_____

☐   Result / resolution of the situation

_____

_____

_____

_____

■ **Tell me about a conflict with a subordinate employee.**

☐   Description of the situation

_____

_____

_____

_____

☐ How I handled the situation

_____

_____

_____

_____

☐ Result / resolution of the situation

_____

_____

_____

_____

Have you ever caused a problem which you later had to apologise for?

☐ Description of the situation

_____

_____

_____

_____

☐ How I handled the situation

_____

_____

_____

_____

☐ Result / resolution of the situation

_____

_____

_____

_____

■ **How do you lead teams to achieve the desired work result?**

☐ Description of the situation

_____

_____

_____

_____

☐ How I handled the situation

_____

_____

_____

_____

☐ Result / resolution of the situation

_____

_____

_____

_____

■ **In which situations do you consider teamwork to be unnecessary?**

☐ Description of the situation

_____
_____
_____
_____

☐ How I handled the situation

_____
_____
_____
_____

☐ Result / resolution of the situation

_____
_____
_____
_____

■ **Have you ever spontaneously taken on a leadership role?**

☐ Description of the situation

_____
_____
_____
_____

☐   How I handled the situation

_____

_____

_____

_____

☐   Result / resolution of the situation

_____

_____

_____

_____

■   **When have you ever not lived up to a leadership role?**

☐   Description of the situation

_____

_____

_____

_____

☐   How I handled the situation

_____

_____

_____

_____

☐   Result / resolution of the situation

_____

_____

_____

Give me an example of your way of leading a team.

☐   Description of the situation

_____

_____

_____

☐   How I handled the situation

_____

_____

_____

☐   Result / resolution of the situation

_____

_____

_____

■ **Give me an example of how you distribute tasks among team members.**

☐   Description of the situation

_____

_____

_____

_____

☐   How I handled the situation

_____

_____

_____

_____

☐   Result / resolution of the situation

_____

_____

_____

_____

■ **Have you ever had to follow a rule you considered to be superfluous?**

☐   Description of the situation

_____

_____

_____

_____

☐ How I handled the situation

_____

_____

_____

_____

☐ Result / resolution of the situation

_____

_____

_____

_____

Give me an example of how you motivate yourself to do tasks that bore you.

☐ Description of the situation

_____

_____

_____

_____

☐ How I handled the situation

_____

_____

_____

_____

☐   Result / resolution of the situation

_____

_____

_____

_____

3.2.6 Handling scenario-based questions

In situational questions, you have control over your chosen example and therefore your answer. However, with scenario-based questions, the interviewer presents the framework for action. They often present situations which pose a decision-making problem. A common scenario is how to handle a Captain who is clearly unable to fly but who still wants to do his or her job. As the First Officer, you have several options: You can a) report the incident immediately, b) work towards ensuring the Captain does not fly or c) do nothing and hope for the best. Option c) is obviously not a good choice. Even option a) does not show very confident behaviour. Flight safety is of course always top priority, but you should give your colleague the opportunity to do the right thing in a sensitive situation like this.

Be careful: Do not beat around the bush. The interviewer knows the actions you could choose. He or she wants to know what precisely you would do in the described situation and why. Your approach must consider the possible consequences of your decision and lead to an acceptable solution of the set problem.

❝❞   **Example**

You are presented with the following scenario in the interview: "Before a ferry flight from Hamburg to Frankfurt, you notice that your Captain has a nosebleed and that he is obviously suffering from a severe headache. What do you do?"

You: *I would ask him if he feels capable of flying.*

Interviewer: *Good, but the Captain downplays the issue. He appreciates your concern but it's just a short flight and he also wants to go home.*

You: *I would say that I was very worried and do not believe him capable of flying. I would urge him to report himself as unfit-to-fly.*

Interviewer: *The Captain still wants to fly. He thinks he is fine to fly and that you, a fledgling pilot, should not interfere. Besides which, there are no passengers on board the ferry flight.*

You: *I would point out that his behaviour is not in line with the company's guidelines and ask him not to put me in a position where I have to make the decision for him.*

Exercise

Write structured responses to the following questions / tasks:

- You fly through a bad weather front over the North Sea. Despite bad turbulence, the Captain wants to go to the Crew Rest Area for a break. What do you do?

- A VIP passenger from Business Class has offended the flight attendants before a long-haul flight. What do you do?

- At the JFK airport in New York, an air traffic controller has given the instructions for starting an aircraft to his child. How would you behave in this situation as a pilot?

- You notice that the Senior First Officer has clearly not kept to the *8 hours from bottle to throttle* rule the night before a flight. Nevertheless, the Captain still wants to fly. What do you do?

- A friend asks you to pull some strings with your contacts at our airline and hire him as a pilot. What do you do?

3.3 Technical questions

Questions on theoretical knowledge are usually asked at the end of the interview. There is a broad spectrum of topics which includes things such as:

- Principles of Flight
- Performance
- Engines
- Aircraft design / aerodynamics
- Navigation
- Meteorology
- Human Performance and Limitations Theory
- Law

Trained pilots should be able to handle these topics well. Applicants yet to undergo training should at least have a general overview of these topics before going to interview. If you will be flying a certain type of aircraft at an airline, you should know more than just the basic information (engines, wingspan, etc.). A detailed knowledge about the systems sets you apart from the other applicants. If the interviewer knows the aircraft themselves, you can also talk about its unique characteristics and quirks.

The technical part of the interview is often no longer carried out by a psychologist, but by a flight instructor from the recruiting airline. A technical specialist interviewer will find out the extent of a competent applicant's knowledge. Answer questions in the technical part of the interview in full, but be concise. This gives the interviewer more time to ask specific follow-up questions to examine your knowledge in more depth.

Example: Technical questions, area: V-Speeds

Interviewer: *Explain to me what V1 is.*

You: *V1 is the maximum speed an aborted take-off can reach without leaving the runway. V1 is also the minimum speed at which it is still safe to accelerate to V2 takeoff safety speed in the event of an engine failure.*

Interviewer: *And how is Vr defined?*

You: *Vr is the rotation speed, which is the speed at which the nose gear lifts off the ground.*

Interviewer: *How are V1 and Vr related?*

You: *Vr is always greater than or equal to V1.*

The interviewer keeps control of the conversation in this example. The introductory task *"Explain to me what V1 is"* must not be misinterpreted as an invitation to discuss V speeds and their relation to one another. During the technical interview you should always stay on a safe path and put the ball back in the interviewer's court with a precise answer.

An important note: Saying *"I don't know"* is never an acceptable answer in the technical interview. Suppose you are asked in what cases medical equipment must be carried on board and you are not sure of the answer. You should not try to answer with a complete *shot in the dark*. You either know the correct answer or you do not. In the latter case, there are a couple of ways to save yourself: *"I am not sure of the precise guidelines for carrying emergency medical equipment. However, these should be in Section K of JAR-OPS 1."* If you really cannot add anything more, look at the interviewer and say: *"I'm sorry, but I cannot answer this question offhand."*

3.4 Asking the airline questions

"Do you have any questions for us after this interview?"

Of course you do. The interview is about selling yourself well at every turn. Unfortunately, many applicants reject this opportunity to round off the positive impression the interviewer has got of them. The interviewer will give you the opportunity to ask questions at the end of nearly every interview. This is not just mere courtesy. The questions you ask give the interviewer just as much valuable information about your suitability as your previous answers. Answering with *"No, I think you've explained everything."* shows a lack of interest and motivation.

Some applicants commit another cardinal sin. It is completely inappropriate to ask questions about holidays and social benefits at interview.

Try to match your questions to the tone of the interview. If the interviewer's questions implied that your willingness to be stationed at a hub abroad would be a key criterion for their decision-making process, ask about internal company programmes for stays abroad. If the interviewer has addressed the topic of good teamwork in the airline several times, ask for his or her opinion on the most prominent features of the corporate culture that promotes this work environment.

Picking up on the focus of the interview with your own (discerning!) questions will always score you points. This shows not only your interest and motivation, but also the fact that you understand the *airline's issues*. You will figure out the best questions to ask if you have recognised the intentions and focus of your interview. With your questions at the end of the interview, you are seeking to:

- Emphasise your motivation
- Highlight your personal suitability for the role
- Demonstrate confidence
- Show that you understand the challenges the airline faces

Finally, you can also ask the interviewer about programmes that help new pilots to settle in during their first few months (e.g. mentoring programme). Be careful not to ask too many questions. Around ten percent of the interview duration is set aside for this section.

3.5 Frequently Asked (Interview) Questions

The following interview questions are real classics in one form or another. Ask a friend to pick out 15 to 20 questions to help you train for an interview situation.

- Tell us a bit about yourself and your career to date.

- How did you become interested in aviation?

- Why should we hire you?

- Why did you choose our airline in particular?

- Have you applied to other airlines?

- What was our share price yesterday?

- Who are the deputies to our chief executive?

- What do you think was the most difficult time in our airline's 50 year history?

- What do you think lies ahead for our airline in the next five years?

- What new routes will we introduce to our next summer flight schedule?

- How long does it take on average for a FO to be promoted to SFO and then Captain?

- What personal achievement are you particularly proud of?

- What makes you a good pilot?

- How would a good friend describe you to a stranger?

- How would you describe yourself in three words?

- What do you see as your personal strengths?

- What would you like to change about yourself?

- Tell me a highlight and a low point of your career thus far.

- Have you ever failed an exam?

- Can you imagine being stationed abroad for a long period of time?

- What will you do if you do not get the job today?

- What would you do if one day you could no longer fly due to medical reasons?

- Imagine that one day you have reached all of the goals you aspired to in your career. What would you give back to the aviation industry?

- Tell me about a difficult decision you have had to make.

- Tell me about a critical situation you were able to defuse.

- What characteristics do you think make up a good team?

- Have you ever had to demonstrate strong leadership skills in order to tackle a problem?

- How do you distribute tasks within a team?

- When have you led a team to a successful result?

- Tell me about a critical situation when you were in the cockpit.

- Tell me about the most challenging crew set-up that you have had to work in.

- How do you behave if a Captain breaches guidelines in the cockpit?

- Tell me about a conflict with a supervisor.

- Tell me about a situation where you had to prioritise tasks.

- Tell me about a situation that you managed to resolve with logical thinking.

- Have you ever used your communication skills to steer a development in your direction?

- What topics keep you and the Captain entertained on a long-haul flight?

- You have mainly flown the Embraer E190 thus far. Tell me something about this aircraft.

- How do you prepare for night flights?

- You notice a slight odour of smoke in the cockpit. What do you do?

- Do you have any questions for us?

Group exercises, discussions and debates

Lots of airlines invite several applicants to a single interview date. This allows them to carry out *group exercises, discussions* and *debates*.

In **group exercises,** you have to solve a task with other candidates under time pressure. Planning or decision-making tasks are particularly suitable for group exercises. For example, variants of the *aid dropping* group exercise are often used. In this planning game the teams have to plan a humanitarian mission in which relief items are dropped at various points. In addition to selecting the most efficient flight path possible, you also have to plan for the optimal loading of the aircraft.

This game shows how systematically individual participants tackle the problems posed and voice their opinions within the team. Applicants in group exercises are assessed on their ability to work in a team and on their leadership qualities.

Technical tasks, such as building a load-bearing bridge from paper, are often commonly used as group exercises.

Different characters and opinions come into play in the group exercises. You are in a competition with the other applicants and want to stand out from the crowd. But you must prove your team spirit at the same time. Here are a few basic rules for group exercises:

- Take an active role in the team
- Bring passive team members into the discussion
- Treat all team members with respect
- Develop your own suggestions for solutions
- Defend your solutions when criticised
- Develop the solution suggestions of other team members
- Give constructive criticism, give a reason for your critique
- Pay attention to the specified timeframe

Teams should work in a results-oriented manner. However, your individual behaviour in the team and contribution to the solution of the task is more important than the overall result of the group exercise.

The same rules apply to **group discussions.** Your team is given a controversial topic that must be discussed openly. Examples for group discussion topics include:

- Should pilots be forced to retire at 60?
- Is the ban on night flights to large hubs really acceptable?
- How do high kerosene prices impact the career opportunities of young pilots?
- Does the EU-ETS (emission trading system) put European airlines at a disadvantage?

Group discussions develop their own dynamics. Be very careful that they do not end in an argument.

A conflict situation is, however, the basis for the third exercise that might await you in the selection process. During a **debate**, your task is to win a conflict starting from an uncomfortable initial position. You should not simply confront your opponent with the situation, but also seek to win them over using well-chosen arguments.

Exercise

Carry out a debate with a partner based on the following situation:

You have formed a band with colleagues in order to relax from your time spent in the cockpit. Your band is very successful and is going to be used for the airline's marketing. However, the marketing department is demanding that the band uses a different drummer. The current drummer has always played very well and was also your personal mentor when you started at the airline. Now you have to tell him that he will no longer be a member of the band.

5 After the interview

End the day of your interview as you started it – with a positive attitude. There is no such thing as a perfect interview. For this reason, you will gain new experience and learn a great deal from each interview. An interview with a German airline will have a different focus than a selection test for a carrier based in the Middle East. Take every opportunity you get for an interview (even if you have already accepted another role).

Write a brief account of your impressions immediately after the interview. Which questions did I answer well? Which questions could I have answered better? Experience is the best preparation. We wish you all the best for your selection test and your career in the cockpit.

SkyTest® Airline Interview

Get to know the structure and process of the psychological interview in pilot and air traffic controller selection tests. The handbook is written by the same authors as this book and presents the structure and methodology of this diagnostic tool, while also viewing the interview from the applicant's perspective.

Recruitment tests for pilots in German and European airlines are modular. During the first stages of selection, applicants undergo computer-based screening tests to examine their operational and cognitive skills. However, it is ultimately the psychological interview towards the end of the selection process that decides whether a candidate is hired or not.

SkyTest® Airline Interview presents the theory and methodology of the interview approach used in modern suitability testing for pilot selection processes. The book uses concise explanations and plenty of examples, as well as biographical and situational sections of the interview from the perspectives of both the interviewer and the applicant.

The interview is a game played against itself. Applicants can be trained how to interpret the questions based on the objectives of the interview and subsequently develop answers reflecting this. *SkyTest® Airline Interview* accompanies you throughout your preparation for this important part of the selection process and provides helpful hints, while a comprehensive catalogue of practice questions allows for direct application.

ISBN: 9783744822510

For further information and to order: **www.skytest.com**